Zeke and th Pop-Pop Bird

Zeke

Blip

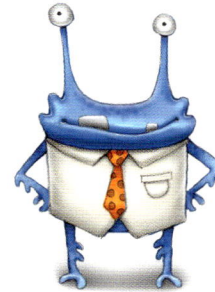

Mr Moon

Written by Jill McDougall

Illustrated by Tom Bonson

Northcott School

"Today we are going to the Space Zoo,"
said Mr Moon.
Everyone got onto the space bus.

ZOOM! Soon they were at the zoo.

Zeke had some popcorn
for the pop-pop bird.
"It likes popcorn!" said Zeke.
"I like popcorn too," said Blip.

Zeke and Blip heard a cry.
They went to find out what it was.

"The pop-pop bird got out,"
said the zookeeper.

pop-pop
bird

"Oh no!" said Zeke.
"We will help you to find it."

Zeke and Blip searched the zoo.

They saw an animal with lumps and bumps.

It was called a lump-o-saurus.

lump-o-saurus

They saw an animal with dots and spots.
It was called a spotty-dotty.
They could not see the pop-pop bird.

Plop! Something fell on Zeke.
"Yuck!" said Zeke.

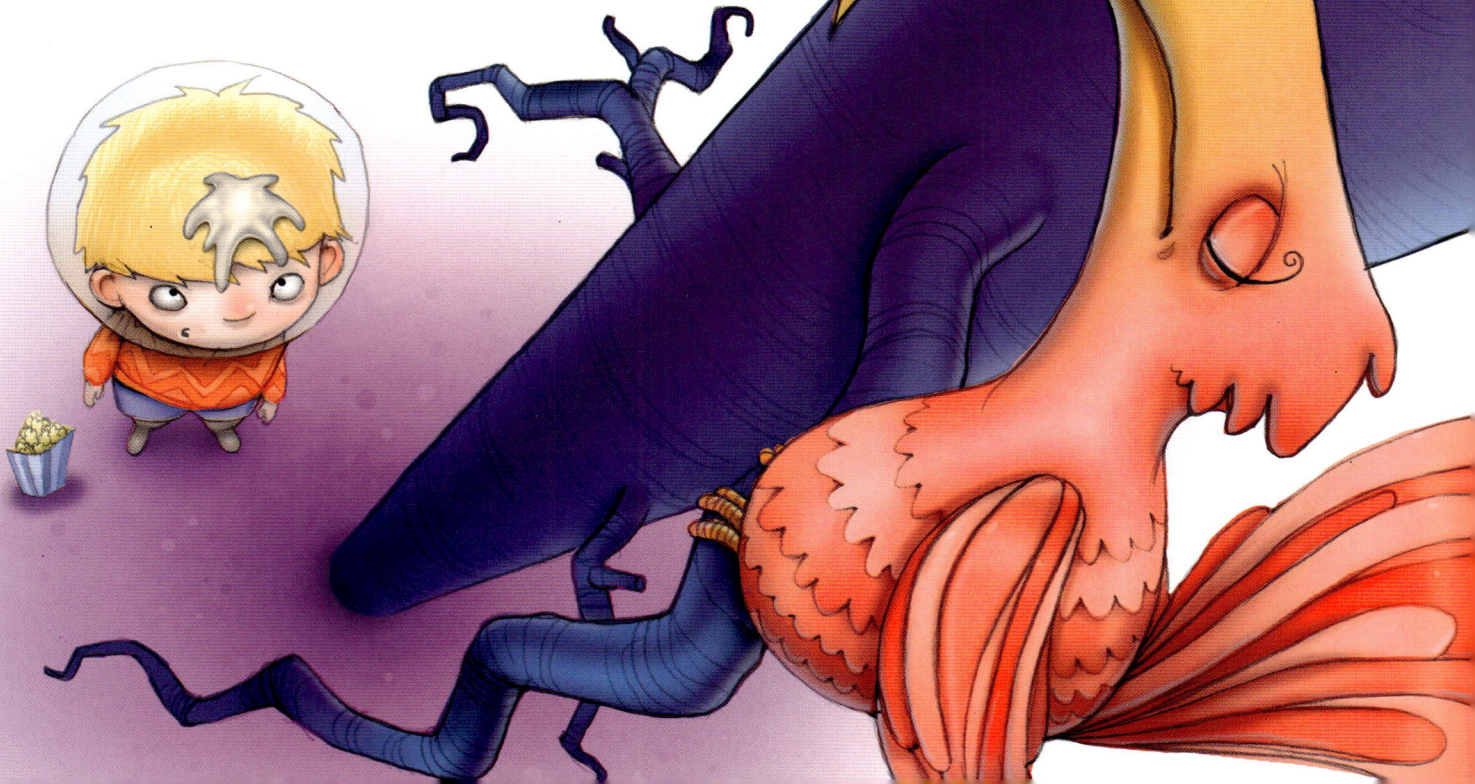

The pop-pop bird was in a tall tree.
It would not come down.

Zeke and Blip had a plan.
They put some popcorn under the tree.
They put popcorn all the way back
to the pop-pop bird's home.

"Come and get the popcorn," said Zeke.

Down came the pop-pop bird.
It ate some popcorn…
then it ate some more.

pop-pop
bird

It went all the way back to its home!

"Good job, Zeke!" said the zookeeper.
"Now let's *all* have some popcorn!"